Praise for the Budgetnista

 Melissa ▓▓▓ Thanks again Tiffany TheBudgetnista! You SAVED my life literally! to some it's may be just money but everything was at stake for me. God bless you!!!

 **The Whole Woman Project** shared your photo.
The Budgetnista is not just telling you how to get out of debt but she keeps it real about her getting out of debt. Love The Budgetnista.

 Allison ▓▓▓ ▶ **Tiffany TheBudgetnista**
1 hr ·

Thanks Tiffany TheBudgetnista you make budgeting and saving so much fun.

 Lauren ▓▓▓ Lol! Tiffany TheBudgetnista, you really have no clue how many times a day your name, or the name of your group is mentioned in this household! You have truly changed the way the hubby and I look at money and credit! I thank you and I hope that people don't scroll past this post but instead actually get involved and get right! ☺

 **Maya** ▓▓▓ @Educ8Money2Kids   12m
Love how @TheBudgetnista defines money. Money is a tool. It can be used to build or destroy your financial life. YOU determine how it's used

 **Rachel** ▓▓▓ @TheBelleAgency   27 Dec
Was able to lower my car insurance today after going deeper into @TheBudgetnista's book. Y'all are sleeping if you haven't gotten it yet.

Praise for the Budgetnista

Lorraine 23 hours ago [LINKED COMMENT]
Oh my gosh! I think you are wonderful!! Come Jan 1 I'm planning on paying down my debt!! You came along at a PERFECT time! Your plan makes so much sense! Your book is on its way!! You are a God send!! I'll keep in touch to let you know how it's going. While waiting for the book I'll be watching your YouTube videos! I'm so excited!!! Thank you for sharing your knowledge! ~Lorraine

Radiant Yes ! Yes! Tiffany TheBudgetnista is defying all types of gender bias, stereotypes, and shattering glass ceilings in the financial advising profession! She getting all bicostal, cross-gender, and multi-socioeconomic..Go head Tiff!!!

Side note: I sincerely appreciate this awe-inspiring group of individuals. ((((Virtual Hugs))))

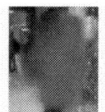
Elizabeth
Today I took the first step in living the way I would like instead of waiting for the lottery to bless me I was able to make a sizeable donation to a friend's business, and I couldn't stop talking about how you helped make it possible, Tiffany TheBudgetnista Aliche! One of my goals this year is to support projects that help us grow as a community. Some people think I have a lot of money, but a little bit at a time adds up to something great!

📱 Like · Comment · Stop Notifications · 3 hours ago via mobile

Latrice Tiffany TheBudgetnista, I just finished listening to your podcast interview and it is inspiring to know that someone just like everyone else has experienced financial hardships that are relatable to ours and is not judgemental; but enjoy sharing your wealth of information to help the rest of us to live or best lives. Thanks!

Praise for the Live Richer Challenge

Khalilah Keep me posted Tiffany TheBudgetnista if they want someone on the East Coast! The whole challenge was a huge blessing for me! The biggest benefit I received from the challenge is a new mindset. My thinking has totally been transformed as a result of the LRC. That is priceless and something that can never be taken away from me!!! #Blessed and thanks again Tiffany for the passionate work that you do!

1 min · Unlike · 👍 1

Chiniqua ▶ Dream Catchers : LIVE RICHER
16 hrs

I've been in this group for a while and never posted anything. Just wanted to share a little today. Before I started the challenge I had a maxed out credit card, all of my bills were past due, I had multiple pay day loans, and a credit score in the 400s. I had a shopping problem and continued to shop and waste money knowing my bills weren't paid. Sometimes I had to borrow money from my mother to get to work. It took an eviction notice and my cable getting cut off for me to wake up.

I found the challenge and it really helped me to get my priorities straight. It took a lot of hard work. I had to cut everything that was not necessary out of my budget. No shopping trips. No spending $15 a day eating out. No buying expensive gifts. I learned to do my own hair and nails. I bring my lunch everyday. I learned how to coupon and actually enjoy being cheap.

I'm finally caught up on all my bills, credit card is paid off, and I even opened my first savings account. It feels so good knowing I don't owe money to anyone and have a little nest egg. Thanks Tiffany for creating the challenge and everyone in the group for all the great advice you post. 😊

LIVE RICHER CHALLENGE. Copyright © 2014

The Budgetnista and its logo, $B, are trademarks of Tiffany Aliche.

No part of this book may be reproduced or transmitted in any form or by any means, electronic or mechanically, including photocopying, recording, or by any information storage and retrieval system without written permission from the publisher. For more information, contact Tiffany Aliche at tiffany@thebudgetnista.com.

Disclaimer:
This book is designed to provide accurate and reliable information on the subject of personal finance, sold with the understanding that neither the author nor publisher is engaged in representation of legal, accounting or other professional services by publishing this book. As each individual situation is unique, any relevant personal finance questions should be addressed with an appropriate professional. Doing so ensures the situation will be evaluated professionally, carefully and properly. The author and publisher specifically disclaim any liability, loss, or risk incurred as an outcome, directly or indirectly, through the use and application of any contents of this work.

Visit the website:

www.thebudgetnista.com

To the Unicorn Squad:

Thank you for helping me make magic happen everyday.

Tiffany

Let's get to know each other.

Hi, I'm Tiffany. Welcome to the beginning of your journey to a higher net worth! If you're ready to develop a wealthy mindset and increase your net worth, you've come to the right place.

"Live Richer" means to purposefully and passionately design the life you deserve. The purpose of the *LIVE RICHER Challenge: Net Worth Edition* is to teach you how to increase your net worth so you can live your best life.

Although I received a financial education growing up, I haven't always made the best money choices. I love to share my story because it proves that no matter how bad a situation may seem, it's possible to dig your way out

Tiffany's Financial Fiascos

1. At age 24, I took a $20,000 cash advance from my credit card and invested it with a "friend." This genius move landed me $35,000 worth of debt a few months later.

2. At age 26, I bought my first home right before the housing bubble burst. The value of my $220,000 condo declined to $150,000 during the Great Recession.

3. At age 30, as a result of losing my job during the recession, I was unable to keep up with my bills. The credit score of 802 I once enjoyed, quickly plummeted to 574.

During that time my net worth was a negative number. Pretty bad, huh? Once I adopted my LIVE RICHER lifestyle, I was able to pay off my credit card debt in two and a half years, make peace with my mortgage lender, and raise my credit score almost 200 points over a two-year period. Within the last few years, my net worth has grown to multiple six figures and I've even been able to travel to over 30 countries.

Now, I use the solutions that helped me during my "financial fiascos" as a tool to guide people like you, who want to do the same.

In 2008, I started The Budgetnista, an award-winning professional and educational services firm. As "The Budgetnista," I'm a spokesperson who speaks, writes, teaches and creates financial education products and services that include seminars, workshops, curricula, and trainings.

I've written a bestselling book, *The One Week Budget* (a #1 Amazon bestseller), teaching readers how to budget their income and automate the process in just seven days. In 2015, I launched the first edition of another #1 Amazon bestseller, *LIVE RICHER Challenge*, which has helped over 500,000 women across the world save millions and pay off millions of dollars of debt. This book is the **fourth** in my LIVE RICHER series.

You can learn more about me and The Budgetnista at www.thebudgetnista.com.

Why do this challenge?

Enough about me. Let's talk about you. Have you ever asked yourself any of these questions?

1. What is net worth?
2. How do I figure out my net worth?
3. How can I increase my net worth?
4. How can I become wealthy?
5. How can I live a more abundant and fulfilling life?

If so, great! This Challenge will answer them - plus more! I even promise to do so in a straightforward way that'll be easy for you to implement. In just 22 days, you'll have a plan to accomplish your net worth goals.

HOW TO READ THIS BOOK

Are you ready to **grow your net worth** like a pro? Good, let's get to work.

How it works:
Each day I'll assign an Easy Financial Task designed to help you get and stay on the road to success.

The daily tasks will focus on the money theme of the week. The weekly themes for the *LIVE RICHER Challenge: Net Worth Edition* are:

Week 1: A Wealthy Mindset
Week 2: Increasing Your Net Worth
Week 3: Maintaining Your Net Worth
Final Day: LIVE RICHER

How to guarantee your success:
- Every morning, read and commit to the Easy Financial Task.

- Perform the task. Don't worry; it won't be hard.

- Get an accountability partner(s). The best way to rock this challenge is to partner up with at least one other person and work together. It'll keep you motivated. You can also reach out to and work with other Dream Catchers (the name I've given to folks working on the challenge), in the private LIVE RICHER **group** at www.livericherchallenge.com

- Go to the www.livericherchallenge.com book resources page to get the Challenge Starter Kit which includes the calendar, worksheets, and other downloadables you'll need to complete this challenge.

- Share your experiences with me, ask questions, and leave comments via social media. You can find me online here:

The Budgetnista Blog: thebudgetnistablog.com
Twitter & Instagram: @TheBudgetnista
Facebook: The Budgetnista

I've also created many awesome resources for you that can't fit into this book. You can find them for *free* at www.livericherchallenge.com.

LIVE RICHER,
Tiffany "The Budgetnista" Aliche

Table of Contents

Week 1: A Wealthy Mindset

Wealthy Mindset Week Goals 15

Day 1: What Does Net Worth Mean? 16
Day 2: Why is Net Worth Important? 20
Day 3: Your Liabilities 22
Day 4: Your Assets 24
Day 5: Calculate What Your Net Worth Is 26
Day 6: Review, Reflect, Relax 29
Day 7: Weekly Inspiration 30

Week 2: Increasing Your Net Worth

Increasing Your Net Worth Week Goals 33
Day 8: Ways to Increase Net Worth 34
Day 9: The Art of Negotiation 39
Day 10: Entrepreneurship 43
Day 11: Investing 48
Day 12: Side Hustles 52
Day 13: Review, Reflect, Relax 55
Day 14: Weekly Inspiration 55

Week 3: Maintaining Your Net Worth

Maintaining Your Net Worth Week Goal 61
Day 15: Find Your Why 62
Day 16: 401(k) and IRA 67

Day 17: Are You on Track? 71
Day 18: Automatic Success 74
Day 19: Your Vibe Influences Your Tribe 77
Day 20: Review, Reflect, Relax 81
Day 21: Weekly Inspiration 82

LIVE RICHER

Day 22: Envision Your Wealth 84

WEEK 1: A WEALTHY MINDSET

THIS WEEK'S GOAL:

To learn what your net worth is, why it's important, and how to develop a wealthy mindset.

Live Richer Challenge: Net Worth Edition
Day 1: What Does Net Worth Mean?

Week 1: A Wealthy Mindset

Today's Easy Financial Task: Learn how to calculate net worth.

How to rock this task:
- Learn the meaning of net worth.
- Write a goal for growing your net worth.
- Speak your desires into existence.

Welcome to Day 1 of the *Live Richer Challenge: Net Worth Edition*, Dream Catcher!

Woot, woot! I hope that you're as excited as I am! Today is the first day of your journey. We're going to tackle the actual meaning of net worth. You're also going to write down your goals. If you're unfamiliar with the concept, don't be alarmed. Net worth is a financial term that gets thrown around a lot, but isn't always defined.

What is Net Worth?
Net worth is the sum of all of your assets subtracted by your liabilities or debts. Net worth is not to be confused with your income. Your income is how much money you earn. Net worth is the value of everything you own (assets) subtracted by your debt (liabilities). Here's the equation:

$$\text{Assets - Liabilities = Net Worth}$$

Remember this equation. We'll be referencing it many, many times during this challenge!

Examples of Assets and Liabilities

Assets
Cash is an asset, but just one type. Assets are anything you own that has value, including anything that puts money into your pocket such as:
- Stocks and bonds
- Real estate
- Land
- Jewelry
- Art
- Cars
- Collectibles
- Investments

Now, let's talk liabilities.

Liabilities
Liabilities are things that you owe other people, and reduces your net worth. Basically, liabilities are anything that takes money out of your pocket.
- Bank loans
- Hospital bills
- Income tax debt
- Credit card debt
- Student loans
- Mortgages and home equity loans

Your Net Worth Goal
Now you know what your net worth is! *Happy dance!* Your next step is to write a goal. Goal setting is a step that should never, ever be missed. To attain the level of wealth that you desire, you must have a clear understanding of the goals you're trying to reach. Your goal should follow these rules:
- Be realistic

- Be a goal that will motivate you
- Be specific and measurable

Here are a few examples:
- I want to increase my net worth by $10,000 by the end of 2018.
- I want to decrease my liabilities by $5,000 by January 2018.
- I want to go from a negative net worth to a positive net worth by December 2018.

Write down your goals on the goal sheet at the end of this task. There's a space underneath for action steps. Leave this area blank for now. We'll fill this out later on in the challenge.

Say It Loud!
Your last task for this first day is to speak the mission of this challenge into existence. There's an unimaginable amount of power in saying your intentions out loud. I have a quotable graphic you should save and share today on your Facebook and/or Twitter accounts to speak your goal of increasing your net worth into existence. Grab the shareable graphic on the Day 1 book resources page of www.livericherchallenge.com.

Check in With Your Accountability Partner(s)
Make sure your accountability partner(s) are still in the game. Don't have one? Then you have a little more homework to do. Find someone to do the *Live Richer Challenge: Net Worth Edition* with. They don't have to be a financial guru, just someone who's willing to do the daily task alongside you. Having an accountability partner is one of the ways to increase your likelihood of success.

You can also head into the Dream Catcher Facebook group to find other Dream Catchers who are working through the challenge. Send a request to get into the group at www.livericherchallenge.com.

If you have any questions, you can reach out to me on social media:
Twitter: @thebudgetnista
Instagram: @thebudgetnista
Facebook: The Budgetnista
Private Forum: www.livericherchallenge.com
(Go to the website and request to join the private LIVE RICHER forum.)

I can't wait to hear what you'll be working on!

Goal Sheet

How to use this goal sheet
Dream Catcher, take a moment to reflect on your overall financial standing. How can you improve your net worth? Where do you wish to be in 3-months, 6-months, or 1-year? Think about your net worth goals and use the space below to declare your success.

My net worth goal and action plan
Dream Catcher, remember that your goal is a declaration of intention. Be specific, be realistic, and set a deadline! I've included examples of both fragile and strong goals and action steps.

My hope is that you will create one strong net worth goal, and by the end of this Challenge you'll have identified three concrete action steps you can take to make the goal happen.

Goal Examples:

Fragile: I want to increase my net worth.
Strong: I will increase my net worth by $10,000 by October 2018.

My Goal _____

Action Examples:

Fragile: I will pay off debt to improve my net worth.
Strong: To increase my net worth by $10,000 by October 2018, I will:

- Action (1) Pay off $2,500 of my student loan
- Action (2) Pay off $2,500 in credit card debt
- Action (3) Save $5,000 for emergencies

Action #1 _____

Action #2 _____

Action #3 _____

I, _____, pledge to work towards achieving the above goal, beginning with the Live Richer Challenge: Net Worth Edition, presented by The Budgetnista.

Live Richer Challenge: Net Worth Edition
Day 2: Why is Net Worth Important?

Week 1: A Wealthy Mindset

Today's Easy Financial Task: Learn how net worth and your spending habits relate to financial freedom.

How to rock this task:
- Find out how a positive net worth can have a HUGE impact on your life.
- Watch a video on how your spending habits impact your net worth and wealth.

Welcome to Day 2 of the *Live Richer Challenge: Net Worth Edition*. Today we're talking about why it all matters. What impact does net worth have on your life? While having a high income is great, earning a lot of money means nothing if you don't manage it well.

It's having a high overall net worth that leads to financial freedom. The idea of financial freedom is being able to do whatever you want to do without having money hold you back. Financial freedom can mean:
- Retiring early
- Traveling multiple times a year
- Going out to eat without worrying that you'll spend your very last dollar
- Saving a sizeable college fund for your children

Some view financial freedom as a "pie in the sky." It's something that sounds great, but unattainable. I'm happy to let you know, that's not the case! You can make sacrifices right now to achieve financial freedom sooner than later. To take this point home, I'm coming to you through video!

Take a moment to watch the Week 1, Day 2 video on the book resources page of www.livericherchallenge.com. You'll learn:
- How making sacrifices by curbing spending can lead to wealth

- The difference between being able to pay for something and truly affording it
- How increasing my net worth has helped me achieve financial freedom

After watching the video, comment below with one thing that resonates with you! Do you have a friend, co-worker, relative, aunt, or cousin who will find this video useful or motivating? Share it with them! Remember to reach out to your accountability partners to encourage each other throughout the challenge. Check into the Dream Catchers: LIVE RICHER group as well.

Today, I learned something new about my net worth. I learned that.....

Live Richer Challenge: Net Worth Edition
Day 3: Your Liabilities

Week 1: A Wealthy Mindset

Today's Easy Financial Task: Add up all your liabilities (debt).

How to rock this task:
- Pull out all your debt balances (liabilities).
- Add up your debt.

Welcome to Day 3 of the *Live Richer Challenge: Net Worth Edition*, Dream Catcher!

So far in this challenge, we've talked about goal setting and what sacrifices may be necessary to increase your net worth. Today is the day we take our first step toward determining where you stand. Woot, woot! Our task today is simple, but it may take some time.

Be sure to set time aside to complete this task, because you'll need your list of liabilities to complete the rest of the tasks this week. In this step, you're going to review all your debts to discover how much you actually owe. Fun times, right? *insert not-so-excited face* Before you roll up your sleeves, a word of encouragement: we all have to start somewhere.

You may be scared out of your mind to uncover exactly how much you owe, but it's a necessary step in determining your net worth. After uncovering what's behind the curtain of your financial life, you can take steps toward financial freedom. The small, initial steps will turn into a spring once you get the hang of increasing your net worth.

Always remember, if you try to avoid addressing your debt like the plague, there's no way you'll be able to cure it.

A Refresher on Liabilities
Just a reminder — liabilities (debt) is any money that you owe including:
- Income taxes owed
- Credit card debt
- Bank loans
- Personal loans
- Auto loans
- Student loans
- Hospital bills
- Home (property) loans **
- Unpaid bills (utilities, etc.)

List out each one of the liabilities you have on the Your Net Worth worksheet. You'll find this worksheet on page 32. You can also get a copy of this worksheet on the www.livericherchallenge.com book resources page Day 3.

Let's Talk About Your Mortgage
A home loan is most certainly a debt or liability, but you don't want to include your entire home as a debt because it's still technically something of value that you own. For this exercise, include the balance of your home loan in your list of liabilities. The equity that you have in your home (your home value subtracted by your loan balance) is what you'll include in the assets section later.

List Yo' Liabilities
Your task today is to ONLY fill out the liabilities column on the Your Net Worth worksheet. Get to it! Remember, the My Net Worth worksheet is on page 32.

Live Richer Challenge: Net Worth Edition
Day 4: Your Assets

Week 1: A Wealthy Mindset

Today's Easy Financial Task: Add up your assets.

How to rock this task:
- List your assets.
- Add up how much you own.

Hey, hey, hey! Welcome to another day of the *Live Richer Challenge: Net Worth Edition,* Dream Catcher.

Yesterday, you listed all your liabilities. If you missed that task, make sure to circle back on it because you'll need it for tomorrow's task. Now, for today… we're going to be using the Your Net Worth worksheet again. It's time to list your assets on page 32.

Your Assets
As mentioned, assets are items you own that hold value. For a quick refresher, here are examples of assets:
- Cash
- Savings
- Stocks and bonds
- Land
- Jewelry
- Art
- Car
- Collectibles
- Other investments

What About Assets You Pay for With a Loan?
If you have a loan against assets like your car or home, for this task, subtract the value from your loan balance.

You will write down the portion of the property that you technically own. Here's the equation:

Property Value - Loan Balance = Asset (Equity)

For example: If your home value is $300,000 and your home loan balance is $250,000, $50,000 is how much equity you have in the home.

****UBER IMPORTANT TO NOTE****
Because you've ALREADY written down your loan amount as a liability yesterday on Day 4, I DO NOT want you to subtract your loan amount twice, once in the liability column and again in the assets column. Instead, write the TOTAL value of your home/car/motorcycle etc., in the asset column of your worksheet. These are called depreciating assets.

Example: Let's pretend your entire net worth is your home and it's worth $250,000, but you owe $200,000. Your net worth is $50,000.

$$\text{Assets } (\$250{,}000) - \text{Liabilities } (\$200{,}000) = \text{Net Worth } (\$50{,}000)$$

If instead of subtracting the total amount the house is worth, you subtract your equity ($50,000), from your liability ($200,000), your net worth will be -$150,000, which is wrong. Got it?

Keepin' It Real With Your Assets
There are some assets where determining true value can be difficult, like Beanie Babies (Dang! I'm getting old), art collections, or antiques. Be realistic here to make sure you're not overstating the value of any assets. There's no benefit in inflating your assets because doing so will only distort your net worth.

We don't want that! Consider the fair market value (FMV) for each of your assets. The fair market value is what your asset would sell for today. Not sure what that amount is?

Do some research online to see how much your assets have recently sold for. For your home, you can use resources like:

- Zestimate
- Re/Max
- Redfin

For your car, you can use resources like:

- Autotrader
- Kelly Blue Book

> Keep in mind that these websites are for estimates.

Go Forth and Write Down Your Assets
Have fuuuuuuun with this task, Dream Catchers! Remember... your assets increase your net worth. Give yourself a pat on the back for every single asset you write down today! These are things that you worked hard for.

As always, be sure to check in with your accountability partner to double check they keep up with our daily tasks. Teamwork makes the dream work, and encouraging each other makes a difference!

Live Richer Challenge: Net Worth Edition
Day 5: Calculate What Your Net Worth Is

Week 1: A Wealthy Mindset

Today's Easy Financial Task: Calculate your net worth.

How to rock this task:
- Calculate your net worth.
- Calculate your debt-to-asset ratio.
- Download your wealth affirmation screensaver.

Welcome to Day 5 of the *Live Richer Challenge: Net Worth Edition!*
This week is flying by, right? We're five days in and crushing this challenge! How does it feel now that you're getting a better handle on managing your net worth? *insert total body roll*

Understanding how net worth works is taking you closer and closer to financial independence. The feeling of being free from money worries is one that I want for you, and the lifestyle you're on the journey to having when you complete this challenge.

Woot, woot! Let's keep going.

Calculate Your Net Worth
For the last two days, you've been writing down your liabilities and assets. Be sure to head back to those days if you didn't complete Day 3 and Day 4. You need to complete the tasks for those days before doing today's task. You should have completed the liabilities and assets columns on the Your Net Worth worksheet.

To calculate your net worth, subtract your liabilities from your assets. Here's the equation:

Assets (what you own of value) - Liabilities (debt) = Net Worth

Put your answer to this equation in the space for net worth on the worksheet. Take a moment to reflect on this number. You may even want to go back to your goal for this challenge and make adjustments. The tasks for the rest of this challenge will be taking actionable steps to increase your net worth! *insert Harlem shake* But, before you go anywhere, you have one more task for today!

Calculate Your Debt-to-Asset Ratio
There's a second equation I want you to do. It's called your debt-to-asset ratio. Your debt-to-asset ratio is a comparison of how much debt you're carrying, compared to the assets you have. The calculation for the debt-to-asset ratio is:

Your Debt / Your Asset = Debt-to-asset ratio

There's another space on the Your Net Worth worksheet to place this number. Of course, the lower your debt-to-asset ratio, the better. Checking your debt-to-asset ratio every so often can keep you aware of how much you're borrowing compared to how much you're growing your assets. If you notice that you're consistently doing more borrowing than saving or investing, you need to make some changes.

What to Do After Getting Your Results
Take a long, deep breath. If you're a recent graduate or still repaying student loans, you may find that you have a negative net worth or high debt-to-asset ratio.

Shooooot, you may also have a significantly lower net worth and higher debt-to-asset ratio if you're in the middle of your career or a higher income earner with a sizeable amount of debt. Regardless of your situation, don't freeze up and don't panic.

> Did you know that I have an online school, too? Yup, the Live Richer Academy. That's where an amazing group of experts, instructors and I share much more in-depth tools and courses to help you. Resources include classes on repaying debt, saving, starting a business, investing, repairing your own credit, side hustling, couponing, manifesting your dream, and much, much more! You can learn more about the Live Richer Academy at www.joinLRA.com.

You being here and taking part in this challenge means you're already committed to moving in the right direction. Go you! I'm going to give you tools throughout this challenge you can use to grow your assets and net worth.

Tomorrow and the next day will be for review and encouragement. Are you a little behind on tasks? No worries!

You have two full days to go back and catch up. How's your accountability partner(s) doing? Remember, if you need help during today's task, reach out to them.

Live Richer Challenge: Net Worth Edition
Day 6: Review, Reflect, Relax

Week 1: A Wealthy Mindset

Today's Easy Financial Task: Review, Reflect, Relax

How to rock this task:
- *Review* this week's tasks.
- *Reflect* on the *Live Richer Challenge: Net Worth Edition* tasks.
- *Relax.* Tomorrow we have our final weekly recap video.

Hey, hey, we've made it to the end of the first week of the Live Richer Challenge! Take this day to review, reflect, and relax. Today is also a great day to check in on your accountability partner(s). Do they need help with a task?

Do they need some encouragement? Do you both need to catch up on past tasks? Go back through this week.

Live Richer Challenge: Net Worth Edition
Day 7: Weekly Inspiration

Week 1: A Wealthy Mindset

Today's Easy Financial Task: Watch the Week 1 Dream Catcher hangout chat.

How to rock this task:
• Watch the Video
• Listen to words of encouragement.
• Complete challenge tasks you missed.

Today's our first Dream Catcher hangout video!
During the video, we discuss the tasks we've worked on this week. We'll also talk about the key takeaways and you'll hear how other Dream Catchers like yourself are working through the challenge. Make sure to check in on your accountability partner. Have they completed the first week of the challenge? Are they ready for next week?

FYI: Today is a good day to catch up on any tasks that you missed throughout the week. (Make *sure* you've calculated your net worth. You'll need it for future challenge days.)

Watch the Dream Catcher hangout at www.livericherchallenge.com under the book resources tab, Day 7: Weekly Inspiration.

Week 1: A Wealthy Mindset Recap Checklist

This Week's Goal: To learn what your net worth is, why it's important, and how to develop a wealthy mindset.

- **Day 1**: What Does Net Worth Mean?
  - ○ Easy Financial Task: Find out how to calculate net worth.

- **Day 2:** Why is Net Worth Important?
  - ○ Easy Financial Task: Learn how net worth and your spending habits relate to financial freedom.

- **Day 3:** Your Liabilities
  - ○ Easy Financial Task: Add up all of your liabilities (debt).

- **Day 4:** Your Assets
  - ○ Easy Financial Task: Add up your assets.

- **Day 5:** Calculate what your net worth is.
  - ○ Easy Financial Task: Calculate your net worth.

- **Day 6:** Review, Reflect, Relax
  - ○ Easy Financial Task: Review, Reflect, Relax.

- **Day 7:** Weekly Inspiration
  - ○ Easy Financial Task: Watch the Week 1 Dream Catcher hangout chat.

Week 1 Reflections

_____

_____

_____

_____

_____

My Net Worth worksheet

Assets

Name	Amount
	Sum

Assets − Liabilities = Net Worth

____ − ____ = ____

Liabilities

Name	Amount
	Sum

Liabilities / Assets = Debt-to-Assets Ratio

____ / ____ = ____

WEEK 2: INCREASING YOUR NET WORTH

THIS WEEK'S GOAL:

To learn actionable ways to grow your net worth by increasing your salary, pursuing entrepreneurship, paying off debt, and more.

Live Richer Challenge: Net Worth Edition
Day 8: Ways to Increase Net Worth

Week 2: Increasing Your Net Worth

Today's Easy Financial Task: Learn the fundamental steps necessary to increase your net worth.

How to rock this task:
- Create your budget and debt repayment plan.
- Listen to the *Brown Ambition* podcast episode: "The Student Debt Show of Your Dreams ft. Financial Aid Expert Angela Howze."
- Learn why saving while repaying debt is imperative.

Welcome to another full week of tasks about growing your net worth. Week 1 was all about fostering a wealthy mindset.

You wrote down goals for increasing your net worth. We also talked about *what your net worth actually is* to clear up any confusion. Then, we touched on the mindset you need to have to become financially free.

This week, I'm going to lay out some steps you can take to increase your net worth. I'm not going to lie, you have a lot to do today, but if you want to achieve your financial goals, it's going to take effort.

If you're willing to do the work, I'm here to help you each step of the way. Let's do this!

How to Increase Your Net Worth
Let's remember the simple equation that we use to calculate our net worth:

$$\text{Assets - Liabilities = Net Worth}$$

Based on that equation, there are two ways to increase your net worth:
1. Increase your assets (items of value that you own, i.e., cash, investments, etc.)
2. Decrease your liabilities (money that you owe and debt)

At a very basic level, to increase your assets and reduce your debts you must:
- **Establish a budget.** A budget gives your money a purpose. A budget can help you curb excess spending, so you have more money to repay debt, save, and invest in assets. These are all things that grow your net worth!
- **Earn more money.** Ultimately, being extremely frugal is not always the best answer to building your net worth. Bringing in more income may be necessary to attain financial freedom.

Today, we're going to focus on getting control of your current finances via a budget, a debt repayment plan, and an emergency savings plan. Then, the rest of the week I'll provide specific ways that you can make more money. Woot Woot! Ready? Great!

I have a bunch of great resources that will knock your socks off, put money in your savings account, and help you destroy debt. In that order!

Meet Your New Bestie - The Budget
A budget is the backbone of your financial strategy. Think of a budget as the root system in the soil that helps a flower bloom. A budget is an anchor that keeps your overall financial plan in place. If you don't have a budget yet, grab the first chapter of my best-selling book, *The One Week Budget.* You can grab it on the book resources page at www.livericherchallenge.com on Day 8. It's my gift to you.

There's a My Money List template at the end of this week on page 59 to help you complete this.

How to Eliminate Debt Like a Pro
Moving on to debt. I used a system called the Debt Snowball method to crush debt. Here's how to implement the snowball method in eight steps:

1. List all of your debts in order from **smallest current balance to largest current balance.** Use the Debt List worksheet at the end of this week as well on page page 60 to complete this task.
2. Figure out how much money you can *squeeze* from your budget to repay debt.
3. Make the minimum payment on all of your debt with the exception of the debt with the lowest balance that you have at the top of your list.
4. Automate all of your minimum payments.
5. Put all excess money you can squeeze from your budget to the first debt with the lowest balance on your list. (I suggest paying the lowest debt off first because early success will trigger an emotion in you to keep motivated.)
6. After the first debt is paid off, apply all of the money you were putting towards your first debt to your second debt.
7. Give your debt plan a TURBO BOOST whenever you can by putting any unexpected money (tax refunds, bonuses, commission, etc.) to the debt.
8. Keep the same system going until you're debt free. Yippee!!!

Let's Talk About Those Student Loans...Yikes!
If you're dealing with student loans, my good friend Angela Howze is a financial aid expert and was a guest on my podcast *Brown Ambition,* with me and my co-host Mandi. Angela is a BOSS when it comes to student loans, and helped me get rid of over $17,000 in student loan debt!

Listen to our "Student Loan Debt" show featuring Angela on the book resources page on www.livericherchallenge.com Day 8 as well. In this episode we talk about:
- Catching up on student loan payments when you're behind
- Qualifying for Public Service Loan Forgiveness
- Paying for grad school

- How I REALLY got my federal student loan forgiven
- And more!

What About Saving?
We talked a lot about debt today. I want to close out today's task by stressing that saving while you pay off debt is highly important. You should be putting away some coins in savings because you'll need to rely on them whenever you're in a pinch.

The best thing you can do is start saving *somewhere* with what you have. The amount will blossom and grow as you stay consistent. Use your new budget aka Money List to help you save. I also have some fabulous savings tips to share from Tara Jones of YourPrettyPennies.com. Here's how to boost your savings:

- **Separate your money** - Have multiple accounts to keep your money divided up. Tara uses a money market account for her emergency savings. She has a checking account where her direct deposit goes for basic debit transactions. She also has an employer retirement plan. It's important to not have your emergency savings or retirement savings sitting in your regular ol' checking account where you can spend it freely.
- **Save your tax refund** - It's tax season! Your tax refund can be a great starting point for savings.
- **Get support** - Making a change is always less fun when you're doing it alone. That's why we have the Dream Catcher: LIVE RICHER forum! Reach out to others in the forum for support and encouragement while you're saving. Having support can give you crazy amounts of motivation!

Not sure how much you need to have saved? NerdWallet has an awesome and completely free tool to help you calculate how much your emergency savings should be. There's a calculator on the Day 8 book resources page you can use that tells you how much you need to save.

Still think you don't have the discipline to save? There's an app for that. Try Digit.

Each week, Digit automatically analyzes your account, looking for money you can save based on your spending habits. The savings it finds is transferred into a Digit account. You get a five cent bonus for every $100 saved every quarter as long as you keep saving. It literally takes **less than five minutes to get started.** I know you have five minutes. Don't wait, begin saving: http://thebudgetnistablog.com/digit. You can also click on this link on Day 8 of the book resources page.

FYI: Digit is free for the first 100 days, then there's a $2.99/month fee.

What's Your Next Step?
Today's tasks are meant to help you build a framework to increase your net worth. The strategy behind building our wealth must include these basic steps:
- Creating a budget
- Creating a debt repayment plan
- Growing your emergency savings

Share what you're working on with your accountability partner(s) as well. Keep in mind, accountability means that you share actions you're planning on taking with each other, **following up to make sure things are getting done!** Is your partner doing what they said they were going to do?

Encourage them!

Live Richer Challenge: Net Worth Edition
Day 9: The Art of Negotiation

Week 2: Increasing Your Net Worth

Today's Easy Financial Task: Learn how to negotiate a raise at your job.

How to rock this task:
- Watch the video on negotiating your salary.
- Research the salary potential for your job title within your industry.
- Identify five skills or qualities you bring to your job that you can highlight in negotiations.

Hey, hey there Dream Catcher! Welcome to Day 9 of the *Live Richer Challenge: Net Worth Edition.* Today is a super fun day in this challenge. Why? We're talking about makin' bacon, cheddah, and Benjamins!

If your current income is making it difficult to invest in assets and reduce your liabilities, bringing in more money is the answer to increasing your net worth.

There's no way to escape this truth: If you're living paycheck-to-paycheck, it's going to be veeeeeery difficult to achieve financial freedom. When we discuss bringing in more income often we first think of side hustles. But guess what?

You may not need to take on a part-time job or start a side hustle right now to earn more money. This fact may come as a relief if your time outside of work is already tied up with family, hobbies, or activities that you don't want to give up.

Instead, you can look to your full-time job to explode your income to new heights.

Research shows that women are less likely than men to negotiate their salary, which means you could be leaving money on the table.

Let's be the change we want to see, Dream Catchers! Be aware that closed mouths don't get fed. You probably won't get more money if you don't ask for it even if you're worthy of a raise. In today's task, I'm coming to you through video to give you tips on negotiating your salary.

I also have great advice to share from my friend Patrice Washington aka the Money Maven, on how to go about negotiating a raise.

Your Tasks Today
1. Watch my video on negotiating your salary first! You can find my video on Day 9 on the book resources page.
2. Research the salary potential for your job title within your industry.
3. Write down five qualities, skills, or successes you've had at work that can help you negotiate your raise.

How to Have Success with Negotiation

Here's an overview of what we discuss in the video:

- **Be realistic:** According to Patrice, you'll have the most success with negotiating a raise if you have proven yourself to your employer. Put plainly, if your performance has been lacking, you've been taking loooooong lunches on the regular, or coming in consistently late, you'll probably have a lot less leverage in negotiations. Work on improving your performance before seeking more money. Also be realistic with how much money you're asking for in a raise. Researching the average salary of people with your job title in your area can help you here.

- **Do an audit of your skills, qualities, and successes on the job:** Dig deep to think of what you bring to the job that your employer can't do without. This step may be hard. Even the most successful women have doubts about their awesomeness. If you have trouble identifying the areas where you're THE BOMB, ask a friend or co-worker. It's often easier for others to see amazing things about ourselves that we can't see.

- **Ask for an appointment and be confident:** Prepare for and schedule an appointment with your boss to discuss your salary. Take this appointment seriously because your demeanor sets the tone for the meeting. Lay out your negotiation points clearly. Practice your pitch in the mirror if necessary.

- **Know when to move on:** It may be time to consider other options if you're in a job right now where there is no salary or growth potential. Here are some things to think about:
    - Does your current employer offer free or affordable training in another discipline so you can transfer to a department where there's more earning potential?
    - Can you seek work within your industry at another company that pays better?
    - Can you go back to school and learn another skill or trade that can increase your earning potential?

Asking for a raise or coming to terms with the lack of opportunity in your present career can be uncomfortable. However, you *should* take comfort knowing there is always time for change! Seek options for yourself through learning, training, and networking. Other job opportunities will present themselves when you have the wherewithal to seek them out. Trust me!

Research Average Salaries in Your Field

There's a wealth of information online about salaries for job titles in different locations. Your second task today is to do some digging around to get a feel for salary averages.

After taking this step, you can go into salary negotiations with realistic expectations. Here are some sites you should check out:

- Glassdoor.com
- Salary.com
- Payscale.com

Share Your Special Skills, Qualities, and On-the-Job Successes

Your third and final task today is to write down at least five great things you bring to your job that you can highlight when negotiating a raise. Do this in the next section.

Five great things about me that I bring to the job that I can use in salary negotiations....

_____

_____

_____

_____

_____

_____

_____

_____

_____

_____

_____

_____

Live Richer Challenge: Net Worth Edition
Day 10: Entrepreneurship

Week 2: Increasing Your Net Worth

Today's Easy Financial Task: Learn how to increase your income and net worth with entrepreneurship.

How to rock this task:
- Learn ways to venture into entrepreneurship for extra income.
- Do a mind map to help you come up with ideas that you can turn into a business.

Day 10 and we're getting into another task! Yesterday, we delved deep into the art of negotiation and how to go about getting a raise from your current job. I had so much fun reading the responses to the video and seeing the special skills that all of you posted in the comments.

These are all valuable skills and achievements that any employer would be lucky to have from an engaged employee such as yourself. **Give yourself a round of applause.**

Despite your awesomeness, the reality is it may not always be possible to get a raise from your present job. And, if you need money ASAP, searching for and landing a new job may take too much time to improve your current situation. That's where entrepreneurship can come in and increase your wealth.

The Benefits of Entrepreneurship
I fell into entrepreneurship after facing a few years of not being able to find a full-time job. From my experience, I can tell you first-hand that everyone (and their momma) has skills that can be translated into a business. Plus, the benefits of entrepreneurship are plentiful. Here are a few:

- **The income is unlimited** - When you start and run your own business, you are in charge of how much money you earn. You set your prices and the amount of effort you put in will directly reflect your earnings. You can increase your net worth by leaps and bounds as an entrepreneur after gaining experience and honing in on a business model that works.

- **You can parlay entrepreneurship into a full-time job** - If you dream about running your own business full-time, being a part-time entrepreneur can be a good way to test out different ideas that can eventually lead into a profitable business.

A fall back option if you lose a job - Let's be real, no job is secure. If you do lose your job, being a part-time entrepreneur will give you some income and possibly a starting point for a business that can replace the income you lost.

Where Should You Start?
Consider *starting a business doing what you already do for a living.* Yup! Pursuing your passion for a business isn't always the right way to go. Passions that people aren't interested in buying may be a tough sell. **Yes, I said it.**

I'm not saying you shouldn't be passionate about your business. I LOVE my business, The Budgetnista! I'm saying that passion isn't enough. It's only one of the pieces to the puzzle of your success. When you start a business doing what you do professionally for work, it's easier to get started because it's a field you're familiar with.

This is how I found my sweet spot. My career was in preschool teaching. The skill I perfected during that time is *teaching*. I used teaching methods and my public speaking skills to start teaching financial literacy and growing The Budgetnista brand.

Here's why this approach to entrepreneurship works...
- If your job is willing to pay you for your skills and talent, then trust me… others will be interested in your skill as well.

- Already being paid by an employer in your craft increases your credibility in the eyes of potential customers and peers in the field.

The years of experience you have in a position and industry makes you stand apart as an expert. Think of yourself as a specialist! Sometimes choosing what business to start is simple:

- If you're highly organized and work as an administrative assistant, you can offer administrative assistant services remotely to business owners and other entrepreneurs.
- If you work in the travel industry i.e. hotels, airlines, etc., you could be a destination expert or travel agent.
- If you're a project manager, you can start a business managing projects independently to companies in your chosen industry.
- If you're a human resources professional, you can consult for small businesses or even employees. Employees may need help getting hired or even need advice on handling difficult situations at work.

Pull out the skills you've learned from your current career and create an awesome opportunity for yourself.

Not Sure What You Can Do?
No worries! I have an exercise for you -- mindmapping. Mindmapping is when you creatively transfer everything that's flying around in your brain onto paper. You don't organize these thoughts right away. Rather, you start free writing and then look back at it for trends that can lead you into a new direction or help you solve a problem.

Here's how to do it:
- Grab a blank pen and paper.
- Draw a circle in the middle of it and write "ME."
- Draw four lines coming from that circle.
- Add circles at the end of each line and then write: skills, qualities, expertise, and passions inside each circle.

- Expand upon the ideas you come up with in each circle.
- Based on the results of the skills, qualities, expertise, and passions, think of business ideas.

Nothing is off limits when you're writing. Don't let self doubt dictate what you put in the mind map either! Need help getting started? You can find a free mind map on the book resources page on Week 2, Day 10. Check out an example from a Dream Catcher below:

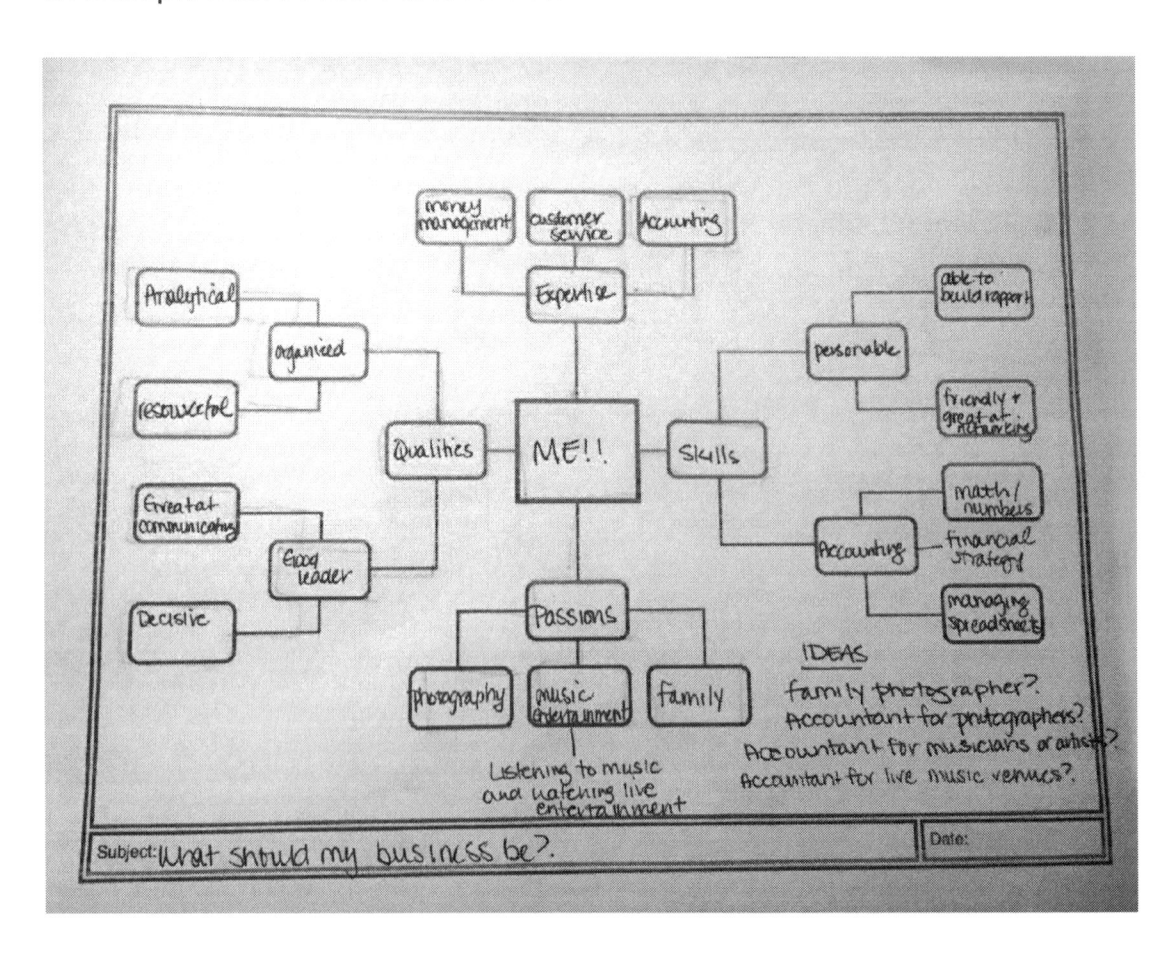

Share Your Ideas

Pick one or two ideas from your mind map and share them with your accountability partner or in the Dream Catchers LIVE RICHER Facebook group. Don't skip this step, because your idea may inspire someone else! Be sure to share what you're doing today with your friends on Twitter!

Business ideas....

Live Richer Challenge: Net Worth Edition
Day 11: Investing

Week 2: Increasing Your Net Worth

Today's Easy Financial Task: Start investing your money to grow your net worth.

How to rock this task:
- Learn why investing is essential for growing your net worth.
- Take one step towards investing today.

Welcome to Day 11, Dream Catchers! Today, I'm going to teach you how to become a beginning investor! Remember how net worth is calculated:

Your Assets - Your Liabilities = Your Net Worth

We've talked about putting money into savings and repaying your debt. It's time to discuss investing. Investing is when you devote money into funds or activities that will earn you returns or profit. Saving cash in an emergency fund for rainy days is very necessary. But money in a basic savings account is an asset that may earn you a very limited (if any) return from interest.

On the other hand, investing in assets like stocks, bonds, retirement funds, and more can increase your net worth exponentially.

Today, I'm going to share two steps you can take to get started investing.

Before moving forward, I do want to mention that investing in anything (stocks, funds, etc.) comes with risk. Please note: the resources in today's task are meant to inform you. The choice of where you want to invest is solely your own.

Now let's move on!

Automating Your Investments With Acorns

Acorns is a robo-advisor that has a very low barrier to entry for new investors. Robo- advisors are systems that automate investing for you after depositing money into an account. Find a link to sign up with Acorns on Week 2, Day 11 on the book resources page of the www.livericherchallenge.com.

Here's how Acorns works:

Acorns invests your change for you. This can add up quickly. You tell Acorns your age, income and investment goals, and the app recommends an investment strategy. Acorns invests your change in ETFs from six asset classes. ETFs are bundled funds that can be made up of stocks, bonds, and other assets. The type of asset mix that Acorns chooses for you will depend on your answers to the initial questionnaire.

How to Get Started With Acorns

Acorns connects to your bank account and automatically transfers money into your investment account. Here's how to get started:

Step 1: Download the app for iPhone or Android.

Step 2: Sign up for an account.

Step 3: Then link your bank account.

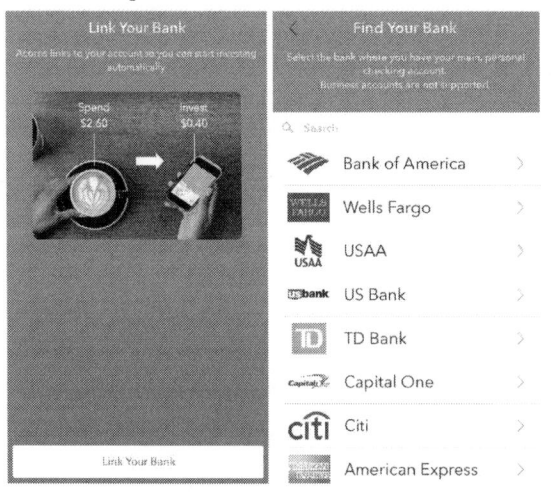

Every time you make a transaction with your bank account, the app rounds your purchase up to the nearest dollar and invests the change.

You can also transfer $5 to $50,000 extra into the account whenever you want!

Acorns is a good way to put a little extra money into investments alongside your other retirement accounts, such as an IRA or 401k that you have with an employer.

Fees: Acorns does come with a fee. Most robo-advisors charge a fee to handle your account, so this isn't out of the ordinary.

If you're a college student with a .edu email address, you can have your management fees waived for four years.

Watch a FREE Stock Investment Q&A

Signing up with a robo advisor like Acorns is a hands-off approach to investing.

What if you want to take a more personalized approach to investing your cash?

I have a solution for that, too! Alanya Kolberg is one of the AWESOME instructors that teaches a course in my school, the Live Richer Academy. Alanya is a self-taught stock investing expert. In her course, **Investing: How to Buy Your First Stock,** she gives you step-by-step instructions on how to:

1. Open an investment account.
2. Choose an investment strategy.
3. Evaluate stocks.
4. Make your first stock purchase.

She recorded a FREE Q&A introduction video about stock investing. You can view her recording on the book resources page on Day 11.

> Enjoy this video? There's a lot more where this came from. In the Live Richer Academy, teachers like Alanya bring you courses on topics like investing, homebuying, starting a business, and much more! Learn more at the livericheracademy.com.

Your Task

Today, you have a choice to do one of two things. You can either:

- Sign up for the Acorns investing app.
- Watch the Q&A with Alanya to get started with stock investing on your own.

This action element is important. Gaining knowledge about investing and increasing your net worth is GREAT, but taking action is what's going to ultimately lead to you building wealth! That's it for today!

Live Richer Challenge: Net Worth Edition
Day 12: Side Hustles

Week 2: Increasing Your Net Worth

Today's Easy Financial Task: Choose a side hustle and take a step towards making income from it.

How to rock this task:
- Learn the great impact side hustles can have on your net worth.

Welcome to Day 12 of the *Live Richer Challenge: Net Worth Edition,* Dream Catchers! We're just about halfway through the challenge. High five! On Day 10, we talked about the benefits of entrepreneurship. Becoming an entrepreneur has changed my life and is a career path that many find as rewarding as I do.

If you enjoy your present career and want to bring in extra money, getting a simple side hustle can take your net worth into the stratosphere. Side hustles are anything you do on the side to bring in an extra source of income.

The Amazing Potential in Side Hustles
My friend Sandy Smith is the perfect example of someone who's excelled at side hustling while still being a boss lady in the corporate world.

Sandy started an Amazon t-shirt business with an initial investment of $500 and earned $25,000 from selling on Amazon that same year!

The lesson here is, don't feel stuck with your current income level. You have options!

Extra, extra bonus: If you're interested in learning how Sandy set up her Amazon store, she has a course for that too. It's on

> Did you know I have a school with a course on how to start your own side hustle? Sandy teaches an entire course on starting a home-based business in the Live Richer Academy! Yup, you read that right! Join the Academy at livericheracademy.com!

her website. You can find a link to her course in the www.livericherchallenge.com resources page on Day 12.

In the course, Sandy can teach you how to:
- Start an Amazon store
- Source products to sell
- Find dropshippers
- Maximize profits
- And much more!

Now back to this task!

The Hundreds Add Up to Thousands
It may take some time to build up your side hustle income, but it's worth the effort!

Take something as small as an extra $200 a week over 52 weeks from a side hustle like taking photo headshots for professionals and real estate agents. *That's an extra $10,400 per year.* Sit back, close your eyes and think about it. What can you do with an extra $10,000+?!

- Can you repay debt?
- Can you invest that money in stock using the information you learned in yesterday's task?
- Can you put money into an emergency savings fund?
- Can you put a portion of the money into your child's college fund?

The possibilities here are endless!

Choosing a Side Hustle
Like entrepreneurship, the best way to choose a side hustle is sticking to what you know. However, there are a few tried and true hustles you can start if you're not sure what to choose such as:
- Babysitting
- Buying and flipping items
- Coaching or consulting
- Dogwalking

- House cleaning
- Housesitting
- Personal training
- Petsitting
- Ridesharing and delivery services like AmazonFlex, Lyft, Uber, and Instacart
- Tutoring

There are plenty of side hustles in this post to consider.

Your Turn
Today's task is for you to think about different side hustle options. We've put a big fat check mark ✔ next to that item on our "to do" list. One more job for you.

Instead of just sharing what side hustle you want to do, I want you to write down one step that you're going to take TODAY to get started with your side hustle. Some ideas:

- **Thinking of dog walking?** Come up with 3 to 4 clients that you can prospect.
- **Want to do ridesharing?** Sign up for Lyft or Uber to get started.
- **Considering housesitting?** Think about how you're going to price your services.

It may be a baby step, but it's a step in the right direction! Don't forget to tell a friend, sister, family member, boss, or co-worker about the challenge before it's over!

Some ideas for quick side hustles I can start....

_____

_____

_____

_____

Live Richer Challenge: Net Worth Edition
Day 13: Review, Reflect, Relax

Week 2: Increasing Your Net Worth

Today's Easy Financial Task: Review, Reflect, Relax

How to rock this task:
- *Review* this week's *Live Richer Challenge: Net Worth Edition* tasks.
- *Reflect* on the components that can grow your net worth.
- *Relax.* In two days, we start Week 3: Maintaining Your Net Worth.

Welcome to Day 13 of the challenge! Hey, hey, we've made it to the end of the second week of the Live Richer Challenge! Take this day to review, reflect, and relax.

Today is also a great day to check in on your accountability partner(s). Do they need help with a task? Do they need some encouragement? Do you both need to catch up on past tasks? Go back through this week.

Live Richer Challenge: Net Worth Edition
Day 14: Weekly Inspiration

Week 2: Increasing Your Net Worth

Today's Easy Financial Task: Watch the Week 2 Dream Catcher hangout chat.

How to rock this task:
- Watch the video.
- Listen to words of encouragement.
- Complete challenge tasks you missed.

Today's our second Dream Catcher hangout chat! During the video, we'll discuss the tasks we've worked on this week. We'll also talk about the key takeaways and you'll hear how other Dream Catchers like yourself are working through the challenge. Make sure to check in on your accountability partner. Have they completed the first and second weeks?

FYI: After watching the video, today is also a good day to catch up on any tasks that you missed throughout the week.

Watch the Dream Catcher hangout at www.livericherchallenge.com, Week 2, Day 14: Weekly Inspiration.

Week 2: Increasing Your Net Worth Recap Checklist

This Week's Goal: To learn actionable ways to grow your net worth by increasing your salary, pursuing entrepreneurship, paying off debt, and more.

- **Day 8:** Ways to Increase Net Worth
  - ○ **Easy Financial Task:** Learn the fundamental steps necessary to increase your net worth.

- **Day 9:** The Art of Negotiation
  - ○ **Easy Financial Task:** Learn how to negotiate a raise at your job.

- **Day 10:** Entrepreneurship
  - ○ **Easy Financial Task:** Learn how to increase your income and net worth with entrepreneurship.

- **Day 11:** Investing
  - ○ **Easy Financial Task:** Start investing your money to grow your net worth.

- **Day 12:** Side Hustles
  - ○ **Easy Financial Task:** Choose a side hustle and take a step towards making income from it.

- **Day 13:** Review, Reflect, Relax
  - ○ **Easy Financial Task:** Review, Reflect, Relax.

- **Day 14:** Weekly Inspiration
  - ○ **Easy Financial Task:** Watch the Week 2 Dream Catcher hangout chat.

Week 2 Reflections

My Money List

MONTHLY TAKE HOME PAY			
MONTHLY SPENDING			
		subtract	
SAVINGS (take home pay - total spending)			
NAME OF EXPENSE	CURRENT MONTHLY AMOUNT	REDUCED MONTHLY AMOUNT	DUE DATE
TOTAL			
SAVINGS (Take Home Pay - Total Spending)			

My Debt List
(NOTE: List debt lowest to highest)

NAME OF DEBT	TOTAL AMT. OWED	MIN. MONTHLY PMT.	INTEREST RATE	DUE DATE	STATUS

WEEK 3: MAINTAINING YOUR NET WORTH

THIS WEEK'S GOAL:

To create a long-term strategy for growing your net worth by finding your why, creating a hands-off system, and surrounding yourself with the right network.

Live Richer Challenge: Net Worth Edition
Day 15: Find Your Why

Week 3: Maintaining Your Net Worth

Today's Easy Financial Task: Find a "why" that will keep you motivated to continue growing your net worth.

How to rock this task:
- Complete the Dream it, Design it, Share it exercise.

Welcome to the last week of the *Live Richer Challenge: Net Worth Edition!* How have you been doing with all the tasks? Have you been enjoying our videos at the end of each week? I am! In today's lesson, we're going to talk about your why through a fun exercise.

The Reason Beyond Finding Your "Why"
During the Live Richer challenges and in the Live Richer Academy, we talk a whoooole lot about money. The goal of the challenges and Live Richer Academy isn't to turn you into a stingy Mrs. Scrooge McDuck who's sitting on a big ol' pile of coins.

It's not all about seeing the Benjamins pile up either. Instead, my mission is to help you build wealth by increasing your income, savings, and investments so you have the means to live your best life. When you see people talking about "living your best life" on the 'gram, you may not be sure what that means for you. Social media celebs and ads try to tell us what living our best life should look like, but only YOU can determine what your best life is.

For today's task, I want you to completely free your mind from what you THINK you should want so you can determine the real why that ignites a fire in you. This why is going to keep you motivated while building wealth.

Step #1: Dream It // Deciding What "Live Your Best Life" Means to You
I want you to do this exercise with minimal distractions. Give yourself 10 completely free minutes to do this and grab a pen and paper. And... I have a worksheet to help you do this! It's at the end of this task!

Here's what to do:
- Close your eyes
- Envision what a day in your perfect life looks like if money's no object. Write down the answers to these questions:
    - What time do you wake up?
    - Where are you?
    - Who are you with?
    - What do you do first, second, and third?
    - How does it make you feel?
    - What major goal have you achieved?

Get as specific as you can with the exercise. Here's an example. Let's say this is the perfect day for Michelle:
- I wake up at 10:00 a.m. because in a perfect world I can sleep in a little bit.
- I'm at home.
- I'm with my kids because I want to homeschool them.
- I wake up, get my kids ready for their lessons, teach them, and take them to extracurricular activities. At the end of the day, I also teach Crossfit at the gym because fitness is my passion.
- This day makes me feel happy, purposeful, fulfilled, and productive because I'm involved in my kids' lives. I'm also healthy, active, and teaching people how to be fit in their daily lives.
- I've paid off my student loans and saved money for my children's education.

Step #2: Design It // Designing Your Best Life
Now's the exciting part. We get to design the life we want.

In this second step, I want you to figure out how much your dream lifestyle would cost you. Michelle wants to be a stay-at-home mom.

If she has a partner who's contributing to the household, she could beef up her emergency savings account, replace her current salary with her own business, and accelerate her retirement savings plan.

She brings in $3,000 net income each month (or $700 net per week).

If her goal is to replace that $700 per week within two to five years, she could:

- Negotiate a raise at her current job so she has more money to save and invest for the next few years
- Start and grow a home based business on the side teaching Crossfit with a goal to replace her income
- Reduce household expenses to grow her retirement savings plan faster (we'll talk about saving for retirement this week!)

We have classes on starting a home based business in the Live Richer Academy (joinLRA.com), if that's something you want to do, too!

See how this works? You may find that achieving your ideal life is actually far more *in reach* than you think.

Whenever you're making sacrifices (i.e. saving instead of spending), close your eyes and think about the lifestyle you're creating for yourself.

Remember the goal worksheet from the first week? There was an action part of the worksheet that you haven't filled out. Remember it's on page 19. Go back to that goal sheet and add three action steps, keeping in mind the designing that you're doing in this task.

Step #3: Share it // We Want to Know Your Dreams!
The last step in this exercise is committing to live for your why, and then share with us on social media and tag me @thebudgetnista!

Dreaming is the fun part. Acting on your dreams takes effort, but it can change your life!

The Dream it, Design it, Share it Worksheet

Step #1: Dream It // *Deciding What "Live Your Best Life" Means to You*

Give yourself 10 completely free minutes to do this and grab a pen and paper.

Here's what to do:

- Close your eyes
- Envision what a day in your perfect life looks like if money's no object. Write down the answers to these questions:
    - What time do you wake up?
    - Where are you?
    - Who are you with?
    - What do you do first, second, and third?
    - How does it make you feel?

_____
_____
_____
_____
_____

Step #2: Design It // *Designing Your Best Life*

Figure out how much your dream lifestyle would cost you.

_____
_____

Step #3: Share it // *We Want to Know Your Dreams!*

The last step in this exercise is committing to live for your why, and then share! Head to our private Facebook Group, Dream Catchers: Live Richer w/ The Budgetnista, and tag me on your favorite social media platforms, @TheBudgetnista.

Live Richer Challenge: Net Worth Edition
Day 16: 401(k) and IRA

Week 3: Maintaining Your Net Worth

Today's Easy Financial Task: Learn about retirement accounts and sign up for an IRA.

How to rock this task:
- Learn the difference between a 401(k) and IRA.
- Request 401(k) information from your employer.
- Open an IRA.

Welcome to Day 16 of the *Live Richer Challenge: Net Worth Edition!* We're close to the end of this week, but there's still a few awesome tasks to get through that will help you grow your net worth! Today, we're going to take a dive into two basic investment accounts — the 401(k) and IRA. Let's dig in, shall we?

What's a 401(k)?
A 401(k) is a company sponsored retirement plan. Companies who offer a 401(k) benefit let you devote a portion of your income from each of your paychecks to the retirement plan. They may also match your contributions to a certain percentage.

You'll often hear financial planners say you should "max out" your employer contributions. This means that you should contribute at least enough of your income each pay period to get the full match from your employer. IT'S FREE MONEY!

When signing up for the 401(k) program, you're able to choose the strategy in which you want to invest your money (stocks, bonds, etc.)

What about taxes?
The money you contribute into your 401(k) is tax deferred. Tax deferral means that your income pretax goes into your 401(k) account. You pay tax on this income later on when you withdraw it at retirement. The good thing about pretax contributions into your 401(k) account is that it reduces your taxable income for the year. Woot, woot for a tax break!

Now... here's the very best part *drum roll*:

Saving money in your 401(k) happens automatically. You tell your employer how much you want to contribute and grow your dough each paycheck without thinking about it.

Can I withdraw money early?
You will get hit with early withdrawal fees if you take money out of your 401(k) early.

I drained my 401(k) when I was in a financial pinch and it was a move I regret. I had to start saving for retirement again from square one and lost a significant amount of the savings I worked hard for because of the fees and taxes.

There are very few (if any) circumstances where you should take money out of your 401(k). Your goal should be to keep money in the account and let it build until you retire.

401(k) Contribution Maximums
The most you can contribute into a 401(k) for 2018 is $18,500. If you surpass this limit, you may have to pay tax penalties so be careful. If you can contribute more than this amount for retirement (or your company doesn't offer a 401(k) plan at all), you can consider opening an IRA!

We'll talk about an IRA next, but first:

Do This Task: If your company offers a 401(k) plan and you're not yet participating in it, request a 401K information packet from your Human Resources department today!

What's an IRA?
An IRA is another type of investment account that anyone who has income to save for retirement can open. It doesn't have to be associated with your employer. You can open up an IRA account at many financial institutions.

Ally Bank is one of my favorite banks! You can learn more about their IRA accounts on the book resources page on Day 16. The two most common types of IRAs are the Roth IRA and the Traditional IRA.

Here's what you need to know about both:

Roth IRA - A savings account where you deposit income that has already been taxed. Basically, you get paid from your employer and transfer some of the cash into the Roth IRA. In this situation, the money you withdraw at retirement is tax-free because you've already paid income tax on the money.

Traditional IRA - A savings account where you get a tax deduction for the contributions you make each year. Like the 401K account, you then pay taxes on this money when you withdraw it in retirement.

How do you invest money in an IRA?
There are two approaches you can take with your IRA account. You can invest the money you transfer into your IRA account manually by selecting individual stocks, etc. Or you can sign up with a robo-advisor that will invest money on your behalf after you choose a risk tolerance you select.

Want to learn how to invest in stock and other in-depth information about investing? We have courses to help you with this in the Live Richer Academy!

Can I withdraw money early?

Like the 401(k), you will have to pay fees if you withdraw money from your IRA early. Again, think of this money as untouchable. You will only be using it in retirement.

IRA Contribution Maximums
The most you can contribute into a 401(k) for 2018 is $5,500. If you surpass this limit, you may have to pay tax penalties so be careful.

Do This Task: If your company doesn't offer an IRA, sign up for one with Ally Bank! You can learn more about Ally Bank IRA accounts on www.livericher-challenge.com Week 3, Day 16.

That's it for this task! Make sure to check in with your accountability partner!

I'm going to do _____ today to start investing.

Live Richer Challenge: Net Worth Edition
Day 17: Are you on track?

Week 3: Maintaining Your Net Worth

Today's Easy Financial Task: Find out if you're on track for retirement.

How to rock this task:
- Use a retirement calculator to determine how much you need to save.

Welcome to Day 17 of the challenge! Today, we're talking about retirement. The golden years. The permanent vacation. Retirement may be years or even decades away from now for you, but early planning is key if you want to live the permanent vacation type lifestyle. The scary truth is, many middle-aged adults are approaching retirement age with little or no savings to fall back on in the golden years.

Here are some alarming stats from The Motley Fool:
- 1 in 3 Americans have nothing saved for retirement.
- The average 50-year old only has $60,000 saved for retirement.
- The average social security check is just $1,355 per month.

Would you be able to lead the lifestyle that you want in retirement on $1,355 per month?

There's also no guarantee that social security benefits will be available for future generations. Ultimately, the responsibility for saving is in our own hands.

A lack of preparedness when you hit retirement doesn't just have an impact on you and your spouse. It can also put a burden on your children and family.

When planning for retirement, you aren't just doing it for yourself. You're doing it for the betterment of your family and legacy.

The time to think about retirement savings is now!

Starting early means you can take advantage of compounding interest. Compounding interest is essentially money, making money, that's making money. We love compounding interest y'all, woot woot!

Since saving for retirement is crucial for increasing your net worth, in today's lesson, I want you to use a retirement calculator to determine where you are right now.

The Retirement Calculator
You can use the retirement calculator from NerdWallet. A link to this calculator is on the resources page on Day 17. Using it is pretty simple.
- Enter your age.
- Enter your household income.
- Enter your current savings.

Use the menu on the left hand side to toggle the variables, including your monthly income, what you'll spend each month when you retire, and your retirement age.

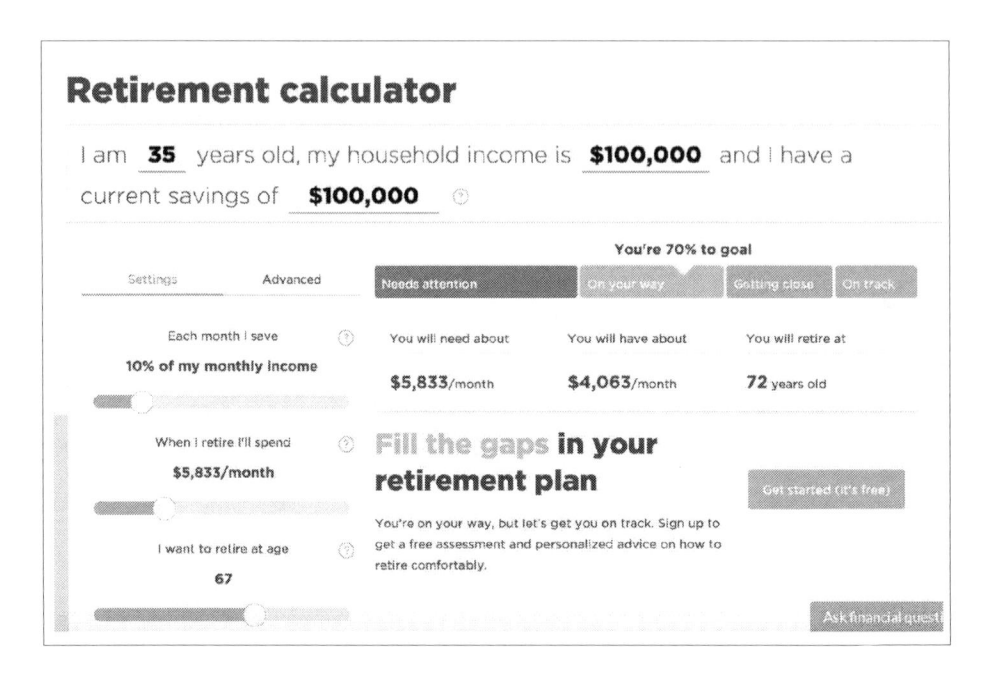

Retirement calculator

I am **35** years old, my household income is **$100,000** and I have a current savings of **$100,000**

You're 70% to goal

| Settings | Advanced | Needs attention | On your way | Getting close | On track |

Each month I save
10% of my monthly income

You will need about **$5,833**/month
You will have about **$4,063**/month
You will retire at **72** years old

When I retire I'll spend
$5,833/month

Fill the gaps in your retirement plan

You're on your way, but let's get you on track. Sign up to get a free assessment and personalized advice on how to retire comfortably.

Get started (it's free)

I want to retire at age
67

Ask financial question

Make Adjustments or Sign up for an Assessment

When you get your result, don't be alarmed if you're not as close as you should be! If you're in the yellow, green, or blue areas, give yourself a pat on the back. You're on your way, getting close, or on track. That's something to be proud of.

If you're in the red and your retirement plan needs attention, take pride in the fact that you're now aware and can take steps to prepare.

We've reached the end of today's lesson!
Woop, woop! I love talking about retirement. Share with your accountability partners how you felt about this task.

My results from the retirement calculator are...

Live Richer Challenge: Net Worth Edition
Day 18: Automatic Success

Week 3: Maintaining Your Net Worth

Today's Easy Financial Task: Learn why automation rocks and how to implement it.

How to rock this task:
- Automate the tasks you've done so far throughout this challenge.

Hey, hey there Dream Catcher! You've made it to Day 18 of the *Live Richer Challenge: Net Worth Edition.*

Today, I want to let you in on my secret weapon for growing my net worth.

Automation!
Automation is the secret that takes the flawed variable out of the equation when you're managing money, a.k.a. You. Instead of having to remember to pay off debt or save, your money will automatically be put into the areas that you decide.

Using this tactic, you won't have to make as many day to day decisions about your money. Instead, you'll put your plan in motion once and then sit back as:

- Your savings grow
- Your investments grow
- Your debt decreases
- Your net worth explodes

The first step to automating is pulling out your budget or Money List. We discussed budgeting and your Money List on Day 8, so you can flip back to that page. Here are a list of things you should automate:

Your Bills
Bills, bills, bills! You need to automate your bills. On your Money List (or

budget) from Day 8, you should see a list of all of your bills. Automate payments for the fixed bills that you can each month such as rent/mortgage, phone bill, etc. For bills you can't automate each month or ones that fluctuate, i.e. utilities that change every month, create a calendar date with yourself. This is a date each month that you sit down and pay bills, such as the first of every month.

Your Savings and Investments
Every payday or once a month, set up an automatic transfer from your checking to savings account. A rule of thumb is to save at least 20% of your paychecks.

In addition to your emergency savings, take advantage of your company's 401k retirement plan if there's one available and match your company's contributions. This is another automatic transaction that can help your net worth grow before your eyes.

If you can't match the contributions right away, no worries! Work your way up to this amount. Make it a goal to increase your contributions by a percentage or half a percentage as often as your company permits. Call up your human resources department whenever you have questions about your company's 401k program. They work for you! Trust me, the feeling of your savings and investments automatically growing right under your nose is one of the most gratifying feelings in the world.

Your Debt Payments
We talked about repaying debt on Day 8 of this challenge as well. We discussed the debt snowball method for repaying debt, which is the way I crushed my student loans. If you need a refresher on it, go here to Day 8 to learn about the method. Today I want you to make sure that you've automated your debt repayment plan. Remember, the snowball method is when:
- You make the minimum payments on all of your debt.
- You focus on your smallest debt first and concentrate any excess money (bonuses, tips, windfalls) to that one.

- When that's paid off, you distribute the money that was going there along with any other money you have to the next debt with the lowest balance.
- You keep going until you're debt free!

What you should automate as far as debt payments is at least the minimum payment for all of your debt. You can also set up a large automatic payment for the debt you're focusing on right now.

Note: I recommend setting up a payment from your checking account and not saving your bank account number into the payment portal of your credit card company or lender. You don't want a creditor having access to your account. Instead, have your bank send them an automatic check each month.

Automation is the Bomb.com
The task today is automate. Don't skip this step. Head to your bank account and set up automations today! Tell your accountability partner when you've completed this task. Accountability partners, ask your partner whether or not they've done the task.

Share what you're doing today with your friends on Twitter!

Bonus: This is one of my favorite books by my favorite, financial author: The Automatic Millionaire by David Bach. This quick read will help you to start to automate your way to a solid, financial future.

Use this section to write down the bills that you plan to automate...

_____
_____
_____
_____
_____

Live Richer Challenge: Net Worth Edition
Day 19: Your Vibe Influences Your Tribe

Week 3: Maintaining Your Net Worth

Today's Easy Financial Task: How to find high quality friends to add to your tribe.

How to rock this task:
- Watch a video!
- Learn why the people around you impact your net worth.
- Learn who to have in your Money Team.

It's Day 19, and we're talking about your circle, your peeps, your crew, your posse.

Why? Even if you're not readily aware of the influence people have on you, you are influenced by your surroundings and relationships. You've probably heard the saying that your income (or attitude) is the average of the people who you hang out with the most. Adding people to your network that are positive, ambitious, and working towards growing their own net worth will be a huge factor in your success.

Today is the last video day, so take some time to head to the book resources page under Day 19 to find out how to create your tribe.

How Can You Increase Your Vibe and Tribe?
Take stock of the people that you have in your life. Do you surround yourself with people who are encouraging and making moves? If you surround yourself with negative people including family and even long time friends, it can be challenging for you to make the change you seek. It can turn into the dreaded crabs in a barrel situation.

Whenever you try to escape the barrel, negative attitudes pull you right back down into the cesspool. It's okay to seek distance from situations that you feel aren't helping you grow personally and financially.

Instead, look for opportunities where you can meet people who have the same motivations and aspirations. The Facebook Dream Catchers forum is one of the first places you can turn to. We also have local Dream Catcher groups where you can meet people in person, too!

Four Things to Look for in a Dream Catcher:

1) **Crystallized focus** - Do they have a clear direction of what they are going to accomplish? Do they remain undistracted by naysayers, lack of support, etc?

2) **Positive attitude** - This doesn't mean they are happy-go-lucky all the time. Do they speak with certainty about their goal? Are they confident that they are able to will and work their dreams into reality? Are they comfortable affirming, "I can..." "I'm able..."

3) **Sickening work ethic** - Anybody can work hard, but are they willing to do the work required?

4) **Elevated company** - Who do they spend time with? Who do they call friend? Are they surrounded by amazing movers and shakers?

Personally, I always try to align myself with people that embody these qualities. The best way to attract a Dream Catcher like this is to be it yourself.

Assemble Entrepreneurial Friends
On top of having friends who have the same financial goals as you, entrepreneurs taking the challenge should assemble a group of other ambitious business owners. Your entrepreneurial group should be full of like-minded people who you can bounce ideas off of who understand your journey as an innovator.

Asking your friends and family for their input on your business can only take you so far. To take you to the next level, you should keep a group of close "big thinking" friends that can hold you accountable to your goals and support your efforts.

My friend Dreena has been my rock since starting my entrepreneurial journey. We both started our businesses in her living room. I was her first PR client! We've fed off of each other's ambition to get to where we are today. Without the love, understanding, inspiration, and motivation we gave each other, there's no way we'd be able to reach the heights we've been able to. Find your Dreena (or group of Dreenas) and you'll be unstoppable!

Create a Mastermind
One of the ways you can get close to other entrepreneurs is by joining or creating a mastermind group. A mastermind group is a group of 3 to 10ish people who agree to meet regularly to discuss goals and keep tabs on each other's progress.

Most masterminds can meet weekly, biweekly, or monthly for a set amount of time. During these meetings, you can recap goals, or even focus your discussion on one person who's having difficulty in their business or needs special support.

For a mastermind to be most successful, you should get a group of people who are at a similar stage in their business that are committed to the process. When all of these stars align, a great mastermind can do amazing things for your business.

Your Money Team
The last vibe to add to your tribe is a Money Team. Who should be on your Money Team? Your Money Team are the folks who are directly affected by your financial choices: kids, spouse, dependents etc., and the folks that help you make financial choices: YOU, accountant, bookkeeper, financial advisor, accountability partner, me ;) etc.).

The key to a Money Team is that you meet regularly (weekly, monthly, quarterly, yearly) in person, via phone etc. Use the results from your meetings to make your financial choices.

One of the most important parts of your Money Team is a group of money experts that can help you reach your financial goals. There's no way you can know everything about investing, saving for retirement, and taxes. I don't know everything either!

That's where professionals come in. They can help you manage your money and reach your goals. Using professionals is worth the investment.

The Cost of Help

Certified Public Accountants (CPAs) or Enrolled Agent (EAs) - CPAs and Enrolled Agent (EAs) are both advisors that can prepare taxes on your behalf. A CPA is someone who can also help you in other areas, like bookkeeping. An EA is someone who's gotten a certification from the IRS to do taxes. If you're unsure of what deductions and credits you qualify for when filing taxes, hiring an expert tax preparer can help you find tax savings each year. A tax preparer often charges anywhere from $200 to $300. *Remember to keep your receipt from tax preparation services because you may be able to deduct the cost of tax preparation the following year.

Chartered Financial Analysts (CFAs) and Certified Financial Planners (CFPs) - Chartered Financial Analysts (CFAs) are specialists in investing and Certified Financial Planners (CFPs) are specialists in all areas -- taxes, insurance, investing, and money management.

There are two primary ways that financial advisors can charge for their services. I'll give you a quick run down here:

- Commission-based - A commission-based structure is when the advisor makes income from referring you to products. At times, commission-based advising can be a conflict of interest. It's possible that your advisor will refer you to certain products because of the commission they'll earn.
- Fee-based - A fee-based advisor charges a flat fee for their services which could be an hourly rate, a flat fee per-project, or a percentage portion of the assets you invest with them.

Some financial advisors can have a pricing structure that has a little bit of both - commission and fees. I suggest you look for someone who's primarily a fee-based advisor because you'll get the most unbiased advice.

Get your crew together! Now, you know the type of people to have on your team.

Live Richer Challenge: Net Worth Edition
Day 20: Review, Reflect, Relax

Week 3: Maintaining Your Net Worth

Today's Easy Financial Task: Review, Reflect, Relax

How to rock this task:
- Review this week's Live Richer Challenge: Net Worth Edition tasks.
- Reflect on the net worth tasks.
- Relax. You're almost done!

Hey, hey, we've made it to the end of the third week of the *Live Richer Challenge: Net Worth Edition!* Take this day to review, reflect, and relax. Today is a great day to check in on your accountability partner(s). Do they need help with a task? Do they need some encouragement? Do you both need to catch up on past tasks?

Live Richer Challenge: Net Worth Edition
Day 21: Weekly Inspiration

Week 3: Maintaining Your Net Worth

Today's Easy Financial Task: Watch the Week 3 Dream Catcher hangout chat.

How to rock this task:
- Watch the chat.
- Listen to words of encouragement.
- Complete challenge tasks you missed.

Today's our final Dream Catcher hangout! During the video, we'll discuss the tasks we've worked on this week. We'll also talk about the key takeaways and you'll hear how other Dream Catchers like yourself work through the challenge. Make sure to check in on your accountability partner. Have they completed the first and second weeks?

FYI: Today is a good day to catch up on any tasks that you missed throughout the week.

Watch the Dream Catcher hangout at www.livericherchallenge.com, Week 3, Day 21: Weekly Inspiration.

DAY 22: LIVE RICHER

FINAL DAY'S GOAL:

To learn how to purposefully and passionately pursue wealth by reciting money affirmations.

Live Richer Challenge: Net Worth Edition
Day 22: Envision Your Wealth

Day 22: LIVE RICHER

Today's Easy Financial Task: Choose money affirmations.

How to rock this task:
- Read through a list of money affirmations you can repeat while building wealth.

Welcome to the final day of the challenge! Throughout this course, you've learned ways to build your net worth. We've discussed technical aspects like paying off debt and saving money. We also talked about investing as a way to grow the dough that you have. You learned what people you need to add to your Money Team, from ambitious friends to professionals like accountants and tax professionals.

Last week, we even discussed your why. Your "why" coupled with the topic today is what's going to help you explode your net worth through the roof.

The Power of Your Thoughts
Here's the thing, you can take initial steps to put information from this challenge to use, but negative beliefs and thoughts can get you off track every time. Your thoughts reflect the attitudes you have about yourself, your income, your ability to grow wealth, and the opportunities available to you.

If you attempt to follow the steps of this course, but you don't believe in your spirit that you're capable of making progress, it will be harder for you to succeed.

Mahatma Gandhi said it best -

"Your beliefs become your thoughts,
 Your thoughts become your words,
 Your words become your actions,

Your actions become your habits,
Your habits become your values,
Your values become your destiny."

Today, in the very final task of this course, I'm going to share with you some money affirmations. Affirmations are statements or declarations that you make to yourself to foster a positive mindset.

If you notice yourself having negative thoughts about your money and building wealth, repeat one or two of the positive affirmations to yourself.

You can also repeat these affirmations to yourself as a part of your morning routine or even the evening before you go to sleep.

Money Affirmations
"I am capable and worthy of building wealth."
"I have access to the tools I need to build wealth."
"I can and will grow my net worth despite past money mistakes."
"Opportunities to make money are limitless."

Do you have any affirmations to share?
These are a few of my favorite affirmations. There are no rules to creating affirmations. You can create a positive affirmation about any part of building wealth that you're having trouble with.

CONGRATULATIONS
You've completed the last task of the Live Richer Challenge:
Net Worth Edition!
Bravo!
Kudos!
Hand claps

Thank you for joining me in this challenge. I had a LOT of fun with you and hope you also enjoyed your time with me and with the other Dream Catchers. The fun doesn't stop here though! We have many more courses and live sessions from experts if you join our Live Richer Academy at www.joinlra.com. It's a school where I provide resources to continue your journey to becoming wealthy and financially free.

The Live Richer Academy Facebook group is also a place that's poppin' all year round with experts and other Dream Builders who are serious about building wealth.

Thank you for participating. You're a rockstar and truly a Dream Catcher!

Twitter: @thebudgetnista
Instagram: @thebudgetnista
Facebook: The Budgetnista
Private Forum: www.livericherchallenge.com (Go to the website and request to join the private LIVE RICHER forum.)

Week 3: Maintaining Your Net Worth Recap Checklist

This Week's Goal: To create a long-term strategy for growing your net worth by finding your why, creating a hands off system, and surrounding yourself with the right network.

- **Day 15:** Find Your Why
  - ○ **Easy Financial Task:** Find a "why" that will keep you motivated to continue growing your net worth.

- **Day 16:** 401(k) and IRA
  - ○ **Easy Financial Task:** Learn about retirement accounts and sign up for an IRA.

- **Day 17:** Are You On Track?
  - ○ **Easy Financial Task:** Find out if you're on track for retirement.

- **Day 18:** Automatic Success
  - ○ **Easy Financial Task:** Learn why automation rocks and how to implement it.

- **Day 19:** Your Vibe Influences Your Tribe
  - ○ **Easy Financial Task:** How to find high quality friends to add to your tribe.

- **Day 20:** Review, Reflect, Relax
  - ○ **Easy Financial Task:** Review, Reflect, Relax

- **Day 21:** Weekly Inspiration
  - ○ **Easy Financial Task:** Watch the Week 3 Dream Catcher hangout chat.

- **Day 22:** Vision Your Wealth
  - ○ **Easy Financial Task:** Choose money affirmations.

LIVE RICHER Challenge Reflections

Acknowledgments:

First and foremost, I would like to give my most grateful thanks to God. He always blesses us. It is we who allow or do not allow our blessings to manifest.

I also want to thank Mommy, Daddy, and my sisters: Karen, Tracy, Carol, and Lisa. You are my cheerleaders, my best friends, my sounding board, and my inspiration. Anyone who knows the *Aliche* girls knows how supportive we are of each other. Thank you.

To all my family, both here and abroad, thank you for your constant love and support. The strong foundation you've provided is the reason I've been able to reach such heights.

Taylor Medine and Tanya Williams, thank you so much for helping me transform and polish my words into a book I can be proud of.

Superman, Jerrell, my husband, thank you for your unwavering support and love.

Thank you to my designer Hector Torres. I came to you at crunch time and you more than delivered.

Thank you, Karen Maine. I literally could not have launched this LIVE RICHER Challenge without you.

Jubril Agoro, thank you for helping me to amplify my voice.

Special thanks to Linda Iferika, Dreena Whitfield, all my family, friends, co-workers, and all of my well wishers.

To the rest of the Unicorn squad, Rachel, Tamara, Sylvia, Lea, Logan, Malea, Nadine, Tamecka and Yheralis, you make MAGIC happen each and every day. Thank for all that you do and give. You're more than a team, you are my sisters.

Lastly, I especially want to thank you. Yes, *you* reading these words. You allowed me to help you LIVE RICHER. You gave me more than I ever gave you. I am forever grateful.

Tiffany "The Budgetnista" Aliche is an award-winning teacher of financial empowerment and is quickly becoming America's favorite financial educator. The Budgetnista specializes in the delivery of financial literacy, and has served as the personal finance education expert for City National Bank.

Since 2008, The Budgetnista has been a brand ambassador and spokesperson for a number of organizations, delivering financial education through seminars, workshops, curricula and trainings. In 2014, Tiffany founded the LIVE RICHER Challenge Movement, a virtual community of hundreds of thousands of women from 50 states and 100+ countries.

Author of #1 Amazon bestseller *The One Week Budget* and *Live Richer Challenge*, Tiffany and her financial advice have been featured in *The New York Times, Reuters, US News and World Report,* Good Morning America, *The TODAY Show,* PBS, Fox Business, MSNBC, CBS *MoneyWatch, TIME, ESSENCE Magazine,* and *FORBES.* She regularly blogs about personal finance for *The Huffington Post* and *U.S. News and World Report* and Black Enterprise.

You can learn more about Tiffany and The Budgetnista at www.thebudgetnista.com.

Made in United States
Troutdale, OR
09/17/2023

12974601R00053